THE ABCs OF METALLICA

METALLICA
HOWIE ABRAMS

ILLUSTRATIONS BY
MICHAEL 'KAVES' McLEER

PERMUTED PRESS

**Dedicated to
Nia, Ruby, Dylan, Quinn, Blaise,
Julie and Donna**

A is for ...And Justice for All,
Metallica's fourth LP,
The first with Jason Newsted,
The new bass devotee.

With Lady Justice on the cover,
"Doris" her funny nickname,
The album was greeted with love,
And lots of critical acclaim.

The songs were a bit longer,
The guitar riffs crunchy and tough.
With drums fast and furious,
Metalheads could not get enough.

B is for the Bay Area,
Up north in the Golden State,
Famous for its giant bridges,
And the corner of Ashbury and Haight.

The Bay is where James and Lars moved to
From down south in L.A.
They went up there to play with Cliff
And then decided to stay.

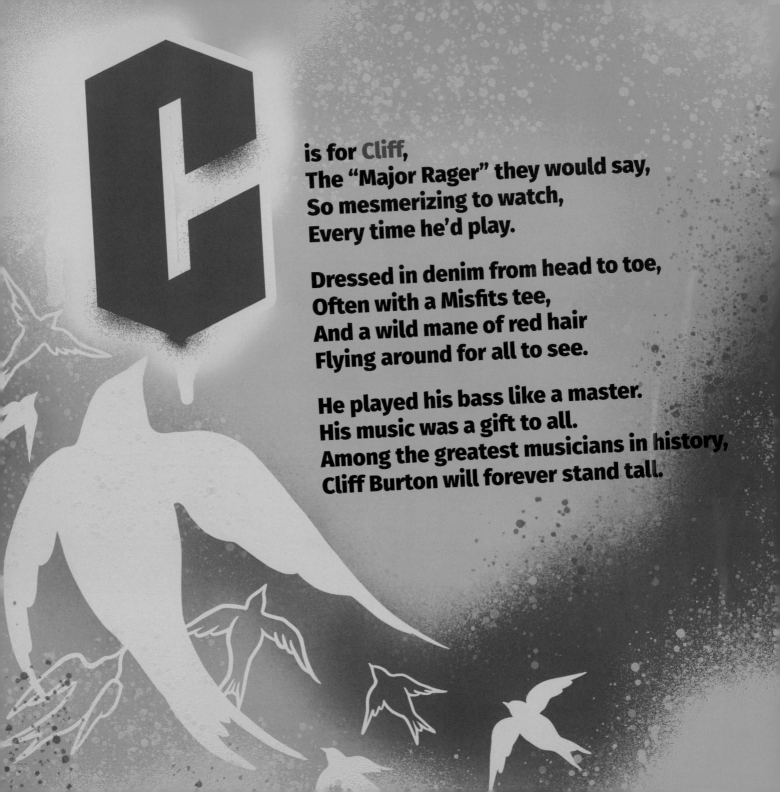

is for **Cliff**,
The "Major Rager" they would say,
So mesmerizing to watch,
Every time he'd play.

Dressed in denim from head to toe,
Often with a Misfits tee,
And a wild mane of red hair
Flying around for all to see.

He played his bass like a master.
His music was a gift to all.
Among the greatest musicians in history,
Cliff Burton will forever stand tall.

is for "Damage, Inc.,"
The final song on album three.
It's also the name of a tour
The group did with Ozzy.

The lyrics speak of honesty
And finding strength within,
Fighting hard for what you believe
And never giving in.

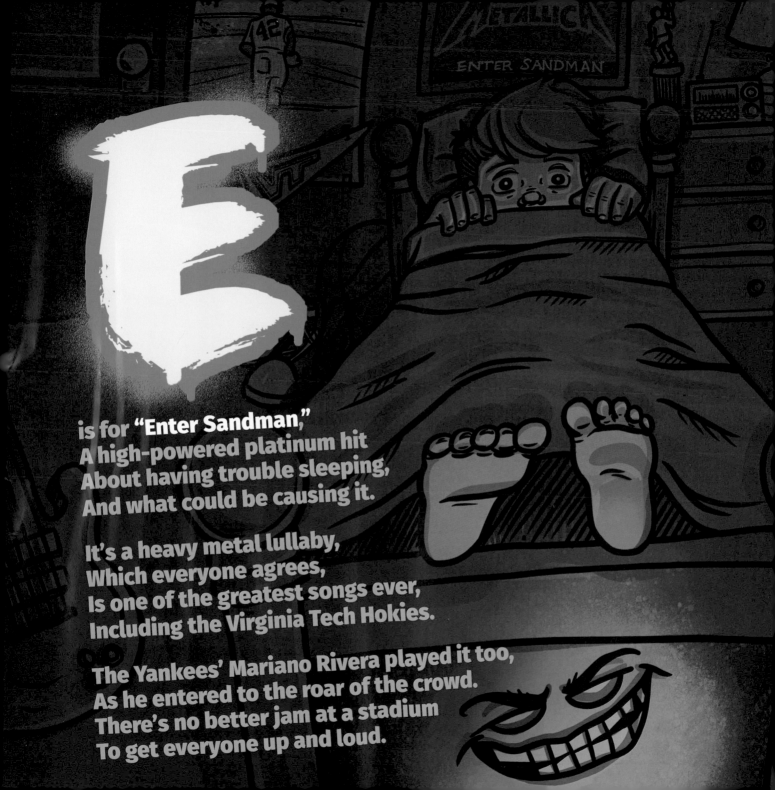

E

is for **"Enter Sandman,"**
A high-powered platinum hit
About having trouble sleeping,
And what could be causing it.

It's a heavy metal lullaby,
Which everyone agrees,
Is one of the greatest songs ever,
Including the Virginia Tech Hokies.

The Yankees' Mariano Rivera played it too,
As he entered to the roar of the crowd.
There's no better jam at a stadium
To get everyone up and loud.

F is for Flying V,
The coolest shaped guitar.
James and Kirk sometimes play one,
The most magnificent axe by far.

Its sound is always heavy,
And it looks great up on stage.
A staple in their guitar racks,
The Flying V is all the rage.

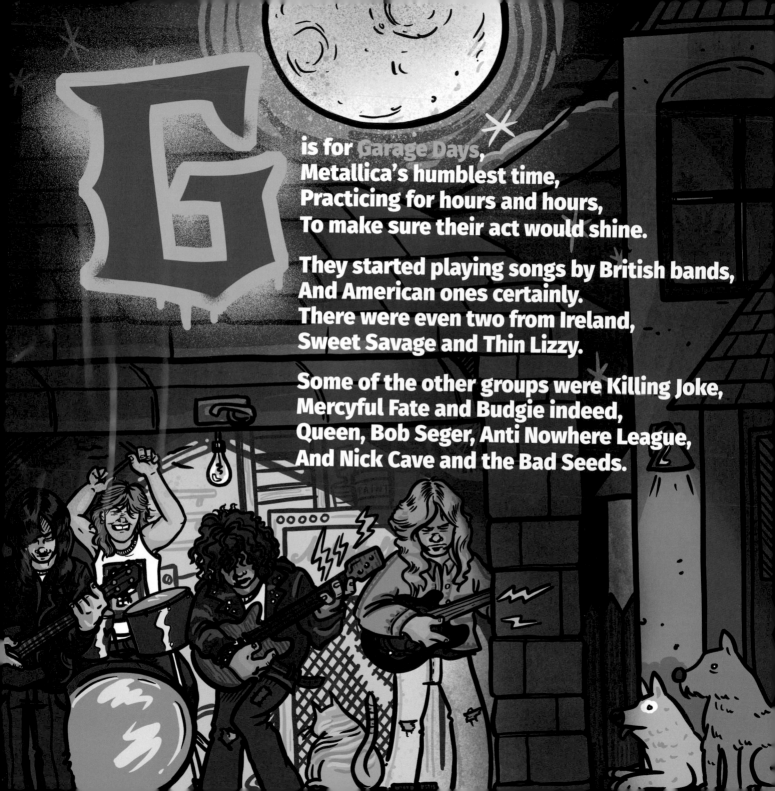

G is for Garage Days,
Metallica's humblest time,
Practicing for hours and hours,
To make sure their act would shine.

They started playing songs by British bands,
And American ones certainly.
There were even two from Ireland,
Sweet Savage and Thin Lizzy.

Some of the other groups were Killing Joke,
Mercyful Fate and Budgie indeed,
Queen, Bob Seger, Anti Nowhere League,
And Nick Cave and the Bad Seeds.

is for **Heavy Metal**,
A sound so loud and in your face,
A tremendous amount of volume,
From drums, guitar and bass.

The look was also quite striking,
With pins and patches everywhere,
Denim, leather, spikes and chains,
And wild, shaggy long hair.

I is for "It's Electric",
A top tune by Diamond Head,
One group that inspired Metallica,
And whose influence was widespread.

There were other bands like Saxon,
Iron Maiden and Motorhead,
Which the fellas became great fans of,
And on which their sound was bred.

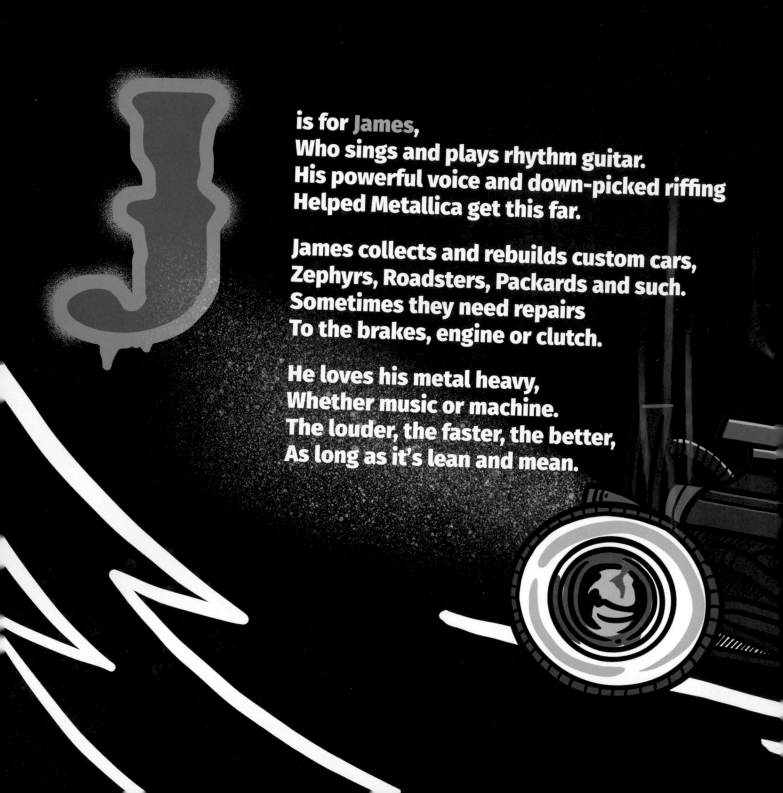

is for **James**,
Who sings and plays rhythm guitar.
His powerful voice and down-picked riffing
Helped Metallica get this far.

James collects and rebuilds custom cars,
Zephyrs, Roadsters, Packards and such.
Sometimes they need repairs
To the brakes, engine or clutch.

He loves his metal heavy,
Whether music or machine.
The louder, the faster, the better,
As long as it's lean and mean.

is for Kirk,
Who shreds on lead guitar.
Lightning-fast with mind-bending solos,
He sometimes uses a whammy bar.

Kirk loves catching massive waves,
Although he never boasts.
He's also thrilled by scary stuff,
Like vampires, zombies and ghosts.

He started in a band called Exodus
Before joining Lars and James
In their little band named Metallica.
The music world was never the same.

L

is for Lars,
Who came from Denmark to play the drums
In the heaviest band ever,
Along with three of his California chums.

Lars loves to listen to Deep Purple
And collects all kinds of art.
He couldn't be stopped once he set out
To help the band get its start.

"Let's play faster than other bands," he said,
"Like Discharge and GBH do."
It worked, and metal fans loved it.
Metallica was on to something new.

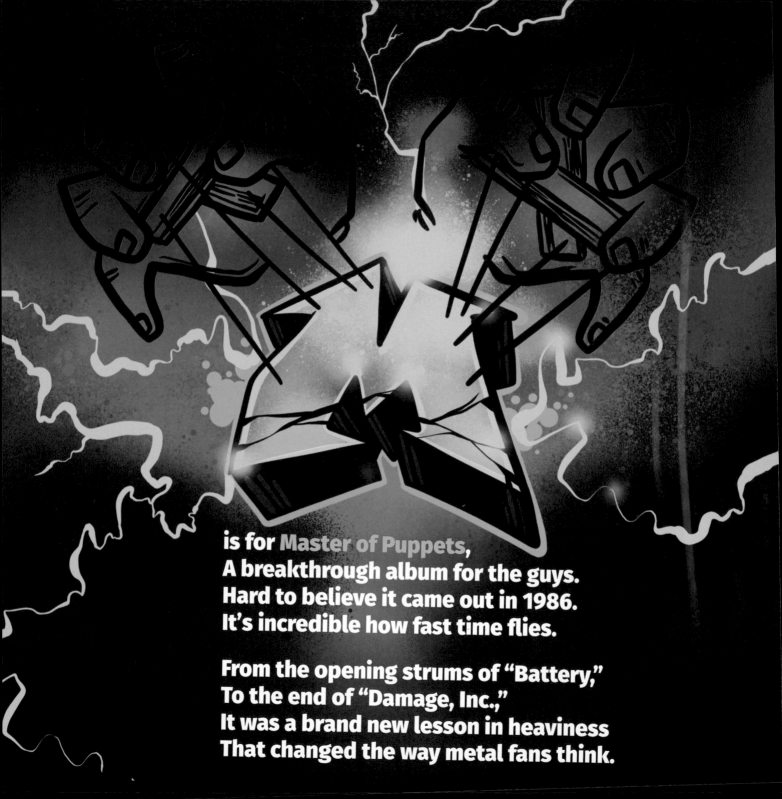

is for Master of Puppets,
A breakthrough album for the guys.
Hard to believe it came out in 1986.
It's incredible how fast time flies.

From the opening strums of "Battery,"
To the end of "Damage, Inc.,"
It was a brand new lesson in heaviness
That changed the way metal fans think.

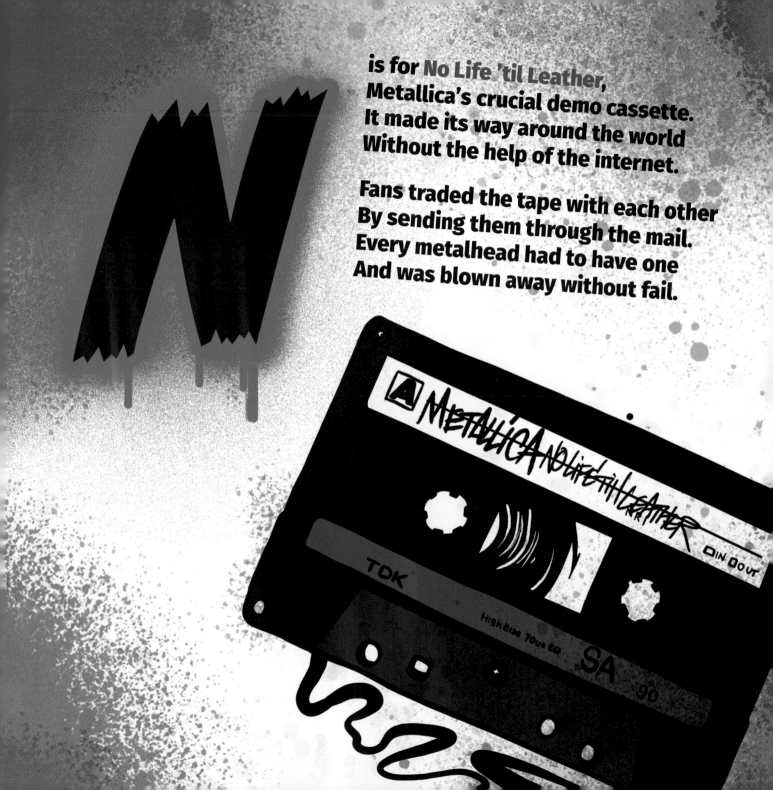

is for No Life 'til Leather,
Metallica's crucial demo cassette.
It made its way around the world
Without the help of the internet.

Fans traded the tape with each other
By sending them through the mail.
Every metalhead had to have one
And was blown away without fail.

is for "One,"
An epic song and music video
Featured on ...And Justice for All
About a soldier's tale of woe.

The track won the band a Grammy Award,
And the video played on MTV.
A grand display of artistry
For all the world to see.

is for Punk,
Created by kids wanting something new,
More riotous and unruly
Than what their parents listened to.

Punk was high-speed and full of mischief,
And its fans looked pretty weird.
With colorful hair and combat boots,
The look and sound has persevered.

Q is for Q Prime,
Metallica's management company.
Some managers work with one band,
And others with two or three.

Management's job is to help the group
With any decision at hand,
From where to tour and which producer to choose,
And to negotiate on behalf of the band.

R

is for Robert,
Who holds the low end down,
With an earth-shattering bass tone
You can feel in any town.

He's a rad surfer and skater,
Slicing waves or carving the street,
A wizard on either type of board,
So agile on his feet.

But Robert's truly at his best
As one fourth of his awesome band,
Touring the globe and rocking shows
Across each and every land.

5 is for Some Kind of Monster,
A movie about the band,
Which followed them in the studio
Before their eighth album was set to land.

Fans got to see how a band works,
With an honest, open view,
The good times and the challenges,
That Metallica sometimes goes through.

is for Thrash,
Underground music played super fast.
When metal bands started playing it,
No one thought it would last.

Many groups increased their tempos,
With furious riffing at rapid speed.
Thrash metal was the newest sound,
For which Metallica helped plant the seed.

U

is for "The Unforgiven,"
A power ballad if you will,
A perfect example of the band's
Thoughtful lyrics and musical skill.

The song talks about growing up
And knowing that you belong,
Always striving to be yourself
And constantly standing strong.

V is for Volume,
As loud as it will go.
You may have heard the old saying:
"IF IT'S TOO LOUD, YOU'RE TOO OLD!"

is for **World Record**,
Which Metallica proudly hold.
In just one year they played on every continent.
Thankfully, gigging never gets old.

They kicked things off in North America,
Then to Europe they went.
South America and Australia were next,
Then in Africa time was spent.

When the fellas looked at the map again,
There was one more place to go.
They finally touched down in Antarctica
To perform in the ice and snow.

is for **X-Ray**,
Which you get when you break a bone.
If you've ever gotten hurt skateboarding,
You are definitely not alone.

James has done this more than once
And wound up in a cast.
He couldn't play guitar for weeks.
Now skating is in his past.

Y is for Young Metal Attack,
Which was written on the band's first tee.
They printed some up for their first few shows,
And now they're a rarity.

The shirt was black and short-sleeved,
With a logo across the chest,
Worn like a badge of honor,
To let people know which band is the best!

is for Jon and Marsha Z,
Zazula, their proper last name.
They heard No Life 'til Leather
And helped ignite the Metallica flame.

They put the guys in the studio,
And their first album was recorded.
Metallica's career was underway.
All their hard work was finally rewarded.

Now you know the Metallica ABCs,
And all the band's great history.

Thank you for your support!

A portion of the proceeds will benefit
Metallica's All Within My Hands Foundation,
which is dedicated to creating sustainable
communities by supporting workforce education,
the fight against hunger, and other critical local services.

For more information about All Within My Hands
Go To: AllWithinMyHands.org

METALLICA

Formed in 1981 by drummer Lars Ulrich and guitarist/vocalist James Hetfield, Metallica has become one of the most influential and commercially successful rock bands in history, having sold nearly 120 million albums worldwide and generating more than 2.5 billion streams while playing to millions of fans on literally all seven continents. The band's several multi-platinum albums include *Kill 'em All, Ride The Lightning, Master of Puppets, ... And Justice for All, Metallica* (commonly referred to as *The Black Album*), *Load, Reload, St. Anger, Death Magnetic,* and most recently *Hardwired...to Self-Destruct,* released in November 2016 and charting at #1 in 32 countries.

Metallica's numerous awards and accolades include nine Grammy Awards, two American Music Awards, and multiple MTV Video Music Awards, and induction into the Rock & Roll Hall of Fame in 2009. In June of 2018, the band was awarded one of the most prestigious musical honors in the world: Sweden's Polar Music Prize. Metallica is currently in the midst of its WorldWired tour, which began in 2016 and is scheduled to continue through 2020.

Howie Abrams

is a former music business executive turned author. He co-authored *Finding Joseph I: An Oral History of H.R. from Bad Brains*, *The Merciless Book of Metal Lists*, *Misfit Summer Camp: 20 Years on the Road with the Vans Warped Tour*, *Hip-Hop Alphabet* and *Hip-Hop Alphabet 2*. He co-hosts a weekly radio show called Merciless with rapper ILL BILL.

Michael "Kaves" McLeer

is a legendary graffiti artist, the author of *Skin Graf: Masters of Graffiti Tattoo*, and illustrator for *Hip-Hop Alphabet* and *Hip-Hop Alphabet 2*. He has created logos and graphics for world renowned artists such as the Beastie Boys and brands the likes of Jaguar and Gretsch Guitars. He is an MC in the hip-hop/rock group Lordz of Brooklyn.

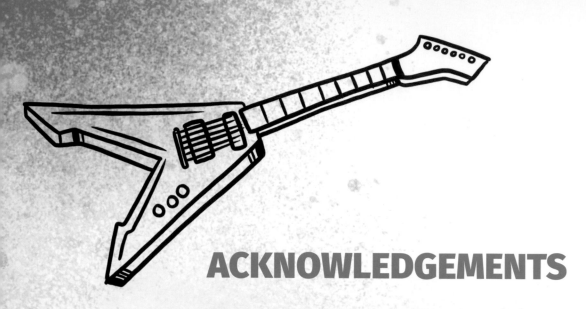

ACKNOWLEDGEMENTS

Metallica would like to express their sincere thanks to Howie Abrams for his creativity and guidance in shepherding this project from start to finish, and to Kaves for his gifted illustrations. Also, thanks to Jacob Hoye and everyone at Permuted Press for their help in making this book a reality.

Most of all, the band wish to thank their immediate families for their inspiration, love and support, as well as the members of the Metallica Family around the world...past, present and FUTURE, to whom this book is dedicated!

Howie and Kaves would like to thank Marc Reiter, Annette Lopez-Lamott, Vickie Strate, Austin Rancadore and all at Metallic HQ, Jacob Hoye and all at Permuted Press, Donna McLeer and especially James, Lars, Kirk and Robert, aka Metallica and the Metal Militia young and old(er) everywhere!

A PERMUTED PRESS BOOK
ISBN: 978-1-68261-899-8

The ABCs of Metallica

Cover and Interior Design by Donna McLeer / Tunnel Vizion Media LLC
Cover and Interior Illustrations by Michael "Kaves" McLeer
Additional Illustrations by Bella Kozyreva
Written by Metallica and Howie Abrams

PERMUTED
PRESS

Permuted Press, LLC
New York • Nashville
permutedpress.com

Published in the United States of America

Printed in Canada